Legendary Moms
Not So Legendary

BOOK ONE

Legendary Moms
Not So Legendary, Book One

Copyright © by Christy Duff

First printing, 2024

To my darling treasures who made every day amazing in one way or another. I'm grateful for every moment that I get to love you and teach you of the beautiful ways of Jesus, and I'm ever thankful for the privilege it is to be your mom.

I love you each more than you could ever know or understand!

Hi friend!

I'm grateful you bought this book, and I wish instead that you and I could hang out together and talk about this over coffee and dessert while our kids sweetly play in the background.

Even though I can't be there with you in person, here's a little study that I taught on this sweet topic; and I hope you feel like we got a little bit of face-to-face time because of it.

You'll also find some written questions and a few pages to journal your thoughts at the end of this book.

Whether you're watching and reading this on your own, as a church group, or with some of your friends; I pray you would feel the breath of God's love, grace, peace, and blessing upon your parenting journey today!

www.christyduff.com/legendarymoms

"Momdemnation"
Defined

Dear darling mama,

Goodness gracious there is a whole lot about parenting that leaves us feeling riddled with guilt, isn't there? One late night when I was (finally) getting ready for bed, I suddenly froze in panic, realizing that I couldn't remember the last time I had taken my three kids to the dentist. Had it been one year? Two years? Surely not three... (I'll just immediately declare this book to be a no-judging zone!) While I was really hoping that I would *actually* remember to call the dentist the next day and make an appointment, I was also terrified at the thought of getting a lecture about the dangers of waiting so long. Compound that with the angst of the dreaded dentist bill that comes at the end of these lectures, and you can see how it was completely understandable for me to be a bit stressed out in that moment. That night I flossed my teeth extra hard as though that could transfer some kind of cleanness upon my children's teeth. As my gums began to bleed, God put a word and a definition on my heart.

Momdemnation: *the condemnation a mom feels with such high demands and varied emotions that are constantly pulling on her.*

There are so many voices out there, telling us what we're supposed to accomplish in this crazy world of 'momming,' yet oftentimes the demands and advice can be in complete contradiction with each other, right? Momdemnation emerges from contradictory parenting pressures such as...

Make sure you have money to get your kids braces, to fix their acne, and to buy them the newest in-style clothes, but while you're doing that, make sure you teach them that the most important attribute in life is that they feel comfortable with who they are on the inside...

You'll also need extra money for sports and music lessons so your children will be well-rounded and learn to follow through, but don't make them participate if they don't want to because you don't want them to feel forced into doing anything...

Teach your kids to eat healthy and be active so they don't become overweight, but don't put too much of an emphasis on diet because you don't want them to be too underweight or end up with an eating disorder...

Your kids need to have a daily, rigorous commitment to the activities they've chosen, but make sure they don't find their identity in what they do because unfulfilled dreams could result in an identity crisis later in life...

Somehow in the middle of all of that daily, rigorous commitment to their after-school activities you also need to fit in a mandatory need for nightly family dinners, because kids who eat with their families have a healthier outlook on life and tend to stay out of prison...

If your kids learn a language before the age of twelve, they'll pick up on it much faster, retain much more of it, and it's good for their brain development; So go ahead and teach them another language really quick between the sports, music lessons, dentist appointments, and family dinners...

Your house should be company-clean in case people drop by, but not so perfect that your family doesn't feel comfortable being there. (Go ahead and let social media bring the torturous difference between desire and reality into your souls on this one) ...

Your kids should go to bed early so they can get enough sleep since they require more sleep than adults and you don't want the cranky monster to take over their attitudes, but make sure you leave a lot of room at bedtime for deep conversations so they can learn to connect with you about their days...

Your kids need to be disciplined so they can learn the reality of consequence, but there are also times to give grace so they can learn that God is a merciful God. You'll need to know when and how to non-emotionally administer the punishment that fits the crime, but also when and how to seize the moment to teach those valuable, deep lessons...

Give your kids freedom because we've all seen how the kids of the strict parents rebel, but make sure you don't let them go too far, because we've all seen how the kids of permissive parents rebel...

Feeling the pressure yet? At this point, I was feeling like the demands of parenting were closing in on me, and I could feel my eyes starting to twitch with momdemnation. There is a condemnation that only we moms can feel and understand, right? Our late-night minds flood with all the ways we feel like we're falling short, and situations replay in our minds like an unwanted T.V. show that we just can't seem to look away from. We ache with all the replayed moments where we wish we would have said something else, done something different, or just plain would have "mommed" better.

Demands, convictions, have-to's, and regrets are non-stop pullers of our heartstrings and attention.

If you're like me, there are moments where the momdemnation feels heavy enough to drown you under its weight. If we focus on what the world says about parenting, or even focus too much on our own expectations, comparisons, desires, and goals we can get ourselves into quite the tizzied mess, can't we? But it's not the times of dwelling in the regretful momdemnation that will get us going in the right direction, and it's not our time spent in immersing ourselves in the guilt driven, regret-filled thoughts that will change our habits or relationships. I've never heard of anyone who has been beat down into being a better person, have you? So how can we find relief in our parenting? Is there anything that can breathe a sigh of relaxed grace into our guilt-ridden thoughts?

In Luke 10 we see Martha having a bit of a 'moment' in the midst of exhaustion and stress. She wasn't a mom, but she did have a whole lot of company at her house, which put a whole lot of pressure and responsibility on her. (I'm sure you've felt that a time or two!) And on top of everything, *Jesus was there!* Can you imagine Jesus being at your house for dinner? Talk about wanting everything to be picture-perfect! We find Martha busy cooking and cleaning for the crowd, and most likely wallowing in the self-pity of being all alone in the kitchen with all the weight of the work upon her weary shoulders. (Does it sound like I have that 'poor me' tone running perfectly through my mind?) I'm sure her thoughts were flooded with how her sister Mary seemed to be having the time of her life, sitting around, listening to Jesus, and though she would have loved to have been right there with her, someone had to fix the food needed to feed all these hungry guys! If Mary would just come help her then she could sit down too, right? And isn't the goal of our day to just be able to sit down for just one moment...(sigh) When Martha's flurry of thoughts finally got the best of her, she came huffing and puffing into the living room, looking for help and pity. (Been there, done that one, right?) But Martha doesn't just have a quiet conversation to rebuke Mary and ask for help. She goes right over Mary's head and demands that Jesus rebuke her sister for not helping her. Sadly enough, I'm thinking it didn't quite work out the way that Martha hoped it would.

"And Jesus answered and said to her, 'Martha, Martha, you are worried and troubled about many things. But one thing is needed, and Mary has chosen that good part, which will not be taken away from her.' "
Luke 10:41-42

Precious mama, I think that Jesus would say the same thing to us today as He said to Martha thousands of years ago. *One thing.* There is only *one thing* that is necessary.

There is only *one thing* that is better. There is only *one thing* that can't be taken away. In those many flooding moments of momdemnation, the question begs to be asked, "Are we choosing that better part?" In a world where so much is pulling at us, are we choosing to listen to the one necessary voice? Are we daily leaning into that *one thing* that will not be taken away from us and is better than any other advice or solution that this world has to offer? Though demands daily pull on us, and pressures daily weigh upon us, the voice of God IS that *one thing* and is available to give us rest.

Sweet mama, I wish I could hold your precious face in my hands today and say to you, "You can't be everything to your kids." You just can't. (Let the tears flow, right?) And even more than that, you were never intended to fulfill that end-all, be-all position in their lives. Love them, play with them, correct them, have fun with them, and enjoy them, but we mamas must remember that their ultimate life direction and every detail in between rests fully in the hands of God. Yes, we have a high calling and a great responsibility as a mom, but it's essential that we remember that the abilities to change a heart, redeem a soul, and use a life greatly belong to God alone. We can pray that they would hear the gospel we lovingly proclaim to them, but we can't be the ones who bring about redemption in their lives. We can pray that their souls would be impassioned by the heart of God, but we can't be the ones who awaken their fervor. We can pray that they would have hearts to serve, but we can't be the ones who call them into ministry.

I'm praying this series of books will breathe a cool breeze of grace into your sometimes scorching-hot world of parenting. Even as I'm typing this, I'm needing to remember God's grace for my last-night parenting foibles. Rest in Jesus. Rejoice in Him. Have fun with your kids. Teach them the good things. Apologize for the bad things. Take a minute. Catch your breath. Praise God for His goodness. And remind yourself that your children's futures don't lie in your hands alone. I'm praying we'll find comfort, peace, and joy through each one of these Biblical moms and their stories, as we remember that our God promises His faithfulness to *every generation.*

Love, Christy

Not So Legendary

Jason and I began our darling fairy-tale of married life together on August 5, 2000, when our beautiful wedding led into a wonderful week-long honeymoon in Hawaii. It wasn't until we had our first night at home in our new apartment that the reality of two people setting out to become one started coming to light. As I reached to turn the lights off, it suddenly sounded like a 747 Jet was taking off in our room. Startled, I turned the lights back on to see what was happening, and Jason sat up to see what my problem was. As I asked, "What's that?" he asked, "What's wrong?" And we instantly ran into a little snag in our new marriage that ended with me saying, "I'm so sorry that your mom put a giant noisemaking fan in your room so you could take a good nap as a baby, but there's no way I can sleep with that louder-than-an-airplane noise every night!" (Any other fan/no fan marriage sleeping problems out there?)

Sleep is a funny thing, isn't it? It's one of our

essential needs as humans, yet we can't seem to make it happen on our own. We all have our personal sleep-well formulas of fans or no fans, special soft blankies, comfy jammies, electric blankets to keep it warm, or blankets with freezer capabilities to keep it cold. We have preferences of soft mattresses, hard mattresses, squishy pillows, feather pillows, hard pillows, no pillows, or five pillows. (Does this sound like a nursery rhyme yet?) We get adamant about things like needing the room to be pitch black while we sleep or needing a nightlight, so we can feel safe in case of emergencies. We have routine requirements of medicine, hot tea, or warm milk to help us fall asleep. For some there are unyielding, unbroken rules of no caffeine, sugar, chocolate, or liquids after a certain time of day because, "otherwise I'll have to get up and go potty!" But then after all that, all we can do is lay and wait, because as much provision as we make to go to sleep, we cannot bring sleep to ourselves. And usually, the harder we try to get to sleep, the more it eludes us, right? God is the only One who can give His beloved sleep.

In much the same way, we cannot bring about our own holiness or purity in life or parenting. Those of us who have tried and found only discouragement or failure can testify to the impossibility of it all. Isaiah tells us that our righteousness is as filthy rags. That means that our best self on our best day still looks like a dirty cloth next to the glorious righteousness of God, and we all know the desperate and helpless feeling of having the stain of sin upon us, don't we? I just want to take a minute to stop and say that if you haven't given your life to Jesus, today is the day! There's no way to remove our sins and have the hope of eternal life without Him. But even if you've already embraced the salvation of Jesus and are gloriously headed for heaven someday, maybe you're still feeling a bit not-so-legendary in your everyday parenting life right now. I'm pretty sure we have all experienced seasons where we feel like failures in our parenting. We all have days where we feel like we just can't hold it all together much longer, but praise God, sweet mama, because *you don't have to!*

Just like the effort we put forth into getting ready for bed, we *should* do all we can do to train our kids in the ways of the Lord. The privilege of making disciples out of them should be a clear priority in our lives. But in all of that, it's imperative that we remember to leave our desired results in the hands of God because we will never be able to perfectly represent Him to our children, and precious mama, *we were never intended to.* In every season, there are moments of 'momming' that make us look and feel good, and moments of 'momming' that make other moms look and feel good about their own parenting skills in comparison to what they perceive ours to be. Usually, just about the time we think we finally have it all figured out is right before it explodes into a sobbing mess of wondering why you ever thought you could be a mom and praying desperately that God would wipe out the memory of that moment from the mind of your kid. (Or maybe that's just me?) God is the only One who can fully put us to sleep, and God is the only One who can perfectly parent your imperfect children.

I remember one night when I had just finished speaking to a mom's group, and a tear-stained mom came up to me. She had recently found out that her teenage boy was involved in something that every mom hopes her child will avoid. Don't those 'finding out' moments spin us off into a world of guilt between the struggles of what we should have known and how we should have handled it? She told me she almost didn't come because she wasn't sure she could handle a 'perfect' mom pridefully declaring how everyone should parent. She was grateful that night for the message of grace that God had put on my heart. Precious moms, shouldn't we all be those who impart grace to each other? If anyone knows how hard it can be at times, it's us, isn't it? No one needs a glance of judgement from a mom who's a legend in her own mind. Let's be moms who instead give each other glances of, "Been there done that," topped with smiles of God's grace, love, and hope. You can't do this Christian mama thing on your own.

The pressure is off, and I really feel like this is a message that needs to be spoken out loud to our souls frequently. There's no magic perfection that enters our hearts when we become a mom. It's usually just the opposite, isn't it? Parenting seems to cause all our sinful, selfish nature to come rising to the surface, reminding us that we are just as in need of a Savior as our kids are.

When I had my firstborn, Haley, and we were getting ready to leave the hospital, I'll never forget my dad looking over at my mom in a tiny moment of panic and saying, "Wait! They're just going to let them take her home?" My dad understood my lack of experience, know-how, and where-with-all as I was beginning down the road of my parenting journey. He kept looking at me with glimmers of tears in his eyes and saying, "My baby has a baby." Oh boy... yep. The baby had become the mom, and this new mom had no clue of the adventure, hard times, and loving moments that lie ahead of her.

I imagine that the Father heart of God feels much the same about us as we continue down the path of this mom-life adventure. I imagine Jesus drawing near with the Heavenly Host, saying, "Look. My baby is trying to raise a baby. Isn't that cute?" Sweet mama, you are just beautiful to Jesus. Your attempts to raise your child in the ways of the Lord are breathtaking to His heart and He's never once thought that you might do it perfectly or been disappointed with you when you don't. Our kids need Jesus, not perfect moms. If we could stand in the place of God perfectly, we wouldn't need Him. And because we can never stand in the place of perfect parenting, we mamas need Jesus desperately every single day!

Isaiah 40:10-11 says...

"Behold, His reward is with Him, and His work before Him. He will feed His flock like a shepherd: He will gather the lambs with His arm, and carry them in His bosom, and gently lead those who are with young."

Precious mama, God is the Leader, the Gatherer, and the Carrier of our sweet little lambs. This verse assures us that those of us with young will be led gently along by His hand. It is with His strong arm that we are carried by His grace. He is the ultimate good Shepherd, and that weight of shepherding never lies upon us even once. We just scoot our kids along with us as we spend our days following that great Shepherd of the sheep.

Our kids are
His flock to feed...
His flock to gather...
His flock to carry...
His flock to lead...

Your sweet attempts to raise your children in the love, fear, and admonition of God are beautiful to Him. Keep it up and press on even further! Good and diligent parenting is a sacrifice of praise unto God. But in the midst of all your attempts and desires, remember that only God can cause a heart to find intimacy in His Presence and salvation in His name. Do all you can, mama, to facilitate their hearts to Jesus, but remember that redemption is up to Him alone, and He will be their Good Shepherd all the days of their lives.

In Zechariah 4:6-10, Zechariah declares...

"This is the word of the LORD to Zerubbabel: 'Not by might nor by power, but by My Spirit,' says the LORD of hosts. 'Who are you, O great mountain? Before Zerubbabel you shall become a plain! And he shall bring forth the capstone with shouts of "Grace, grace to it!" Moreover the word of the LORD came to me, saying: "The hands of Zerubbabel have laid the foundation of this temple; His hands shall also finish it. Then you will know that the LORD of hosts has sent Me to you. For who has despised the day of small things?"

It seems like Zechariah was possibly having one of those days where his vision was filled with the mountains of problems in front of him, and I think every parent can say, "Been there, done that," right? Whether it's a mountain of laundry, a pile of dishes, or a mound of bad attitudes and regrets, we've all faced those days where the mountains in front of us seem to mock our lack of legendary might and skill. So how do we push through and continue to train our kids in the ways of Jesus when it seems like we aren't getting very far or being very successful? How do we make our days about the love of God rather than letting our thoughts succumb to the massive mountains that seem to surround our daily parenting life? I think we get a good picture of the how-to as God comes to Zechariah in the middle of his mountain-filled day.

If you read all of Zechariah 4, an angel is showing different objects to Zechariah, asking him if he knows what they are. Zechariah's answer is always the same, "No, my lord." Zechariah has no idea what he's looking at, and I don't know about you, but there are days in parenting where I feel like I'm walking around with foggy vision thinking, "What is this, and what am I supposed to do with it?" The beauty of Zechariah 4 is that God wasn't intentionally pointing out Zechariah's confusion just to make him feel dumb. This angel was drawing things to light that Zechariah didn't understand, for the sole purpose of speaking wisdom into the picture and causing him to understand the answers. God prompted the questions so that Zechariah could leave the foggy visions with more clarity, wisdom, and understanding than he had before. There will always be situations with our kids where God desires to do a work and it usually begins with Him showing us a mountain of problems. We make the mistake, though, when we think we've been shown the problems so that we can worry about them and try to fix it with our own (not so) legendary strength.

Our days can quickly become a mountain range, can't they? There's a little rock of an attitude here, a boulder of an argument there, a pile of stress, a wall of bitterness, and a heap of, "no one ever says thank you." Out near the desert where I live there's a funny little area called Salvation Mountain and it's actually a mountain of trash and debris that someone covered up with paint and Bible verses and turned into a tourist attraction. If we aren't careful our hearts and homes can become the same. It's interesting and fun for sure to see the way this man has sought to make a giant mountain of trash beautiful, but at the end of the visit you feel like you visited a reformed pile of trash, *because you have.* Sometimes that can be our tendency in parenting. We don't know what to do with all this stuff that has built up over time, so we try to slap some paint and a Bible verse on it and call it a day. But Jesus has so much more for us than that.

We were never intended by God to try and cover up our own mountains or to grab shovels in an attempt to hack them all to pieces ourselves. When we try to make our own mountains into plains, we just end up with bigger mountains and bigger messes. God opens our eyes to the mountains so that we can be those legendary moms who have learned in time to run in prayer to the Mountain Mover. We're shown the problems so that we can soften the ground in prayer while our mighty God levels the mountain. God will often show us a character flaw in our kids or a concerning area in their lives, and He uses our feelings of desperation and inadequacy to cause us to run to Him with our frantic question of "What is this?" We will find our God when we seek Him, and He will always be ready with the answers of how He's planned to fix it all before the foundations of the earth. Mountains are not to be reformed by our own legendary might and power; they are to be leveled by the truly legendary power of the Holy Spirit.

Because every day can quickly become a mountain, we need time every day with the Mountain Leveler. Like the promise given for Zechariah to proclaim, He wants to make our mountains into a plain. As we spend time with Him praying over our mountains and gaining wisdom from Him and the examples He's placed within His Word, He levels those mountains in our hearts, minds, relationships, and realities. He renews our energy and uplifts our weary hearts. It's essential as moms that we realize our times with Jesus in prayer and reading the Word are the most legendary examples we can pass on to the coming generations. It's the everyday version of putting our own oxygen masks on first so that we can then assist our kids. Our times spent with Jesus in prayer for our family are more legendary than any brownies we could make for a bake sale, any science project we could work on, any learning toy we could ever buy, or any expensive prom dress that we could ever shop for. Our legends aren't determined by what we do, our legends are determined by what we let God do in and through us.

The heart of this book series isn't to elevate us into some kind of superhero-mom status. These Biblical moms that we'll be studying weren't legendary because they had it all together. They were legendary because they either learned to look to God for all they needed, or they chose not to. In the lives of these moms, it was either the hand of God upon them that made them great examples, or it was the refusal of the hand of God upon them that made them lessons worth learning from, and for most of them, it was a little of both. The kind of godly, legendary mom we desire to be isn't a perfect mom who makes the right choices every time, but rather she's one who leans into the perfect, loving presence of God each day and teaches her kids to do the same. Let's be the moms who are remembered for loving God with all of our heart, soul, mind, and strength, and then aspiring to teach the next generations to do the same.

1. What areas of motherhood seem to bring about the most pressure for you? Would you say that the pressure comes from yourself or someone else? In what ways? Are there any Bible verses you can find or think of that apply to these specific areas?

2. What would you say your goal is in your parenting? If you could pick just one thing you want your kids to know by the time they're adults, what would it be? In this particular season of your life, what are some realistic steps you can take to aim your parenting toward that goal?

3. What are some practical ways you can remind yourself throughout the day to focus on the "One Thing" of Jesus? (Luke 10:42) How does focusing on Him throughout our day impact and change our parenting?

4. Write out Isaiah 40:10-11. How do these verses encourage you in your parenting journey?

5. Read 2 Corinthians 9:6-13. These verses are talking about giving to support the Kingdom of God, but how could this concept of sowing abundant seed also apply to us parents as we seek to disciple our children?

6. What are the "parenting mountains" that tend to overwhelm you? Is there anything you remember from this book or Bible study that God could use to help level those mountains in your life?

7. Take some time to pray over your parenting regrets and hopes. List them if you feel like writing them down. Think of these prayers as a beautiful bouquet of flowers, and lift them to God, who alone can forgive, make new, lead us as parents, and fulfill our desires for our children.

Do you feel like journaling any thoughts, verses, or prayers?

Do you feel like journaling any thoughts, verses, or prayers?

Do you feel like journaling any thoughts, verses, or prayers?

Do you feel like journaling any thoughts, verses, or prayers?

Do you feel like journaling any thoughts, verses, or prayers?

Do you feel like journaling any thoughts, verses, or prayers?

Made in the USA
Columbia, SC
09 November 2024

45677455R00024